Science
in the
Renaissance

Lisa Mullins

Crabtree Publishing Company
www.crabtreebooks.com

Author: Lisa Mullins
Editor-in-Chief: Lionel Bender
Editors: Lynn Peppas, Simon Adams
Proofreader: Crystal Sikkens
Project coordinator: Robert Walker
Photo research: Susannah Jayes
Design concept: Robert MacGregor
Designer: Malcolm Smythe
Production coordinator: Margaret Amy Salter
Production: Kim Richardson
Prepress technician: Margaret Amy Salter
Print coordinator: Katherine Berti

With thanks to First Folio.

Thank you to Elizabeth Smith, Darwin Correspondence
Project, UK; and Katherine Ireland, Halifax, Canada.

Cover photo: Copper engraving by Joan Galle after the
original drawing by Stradanus (1523-1605).

Photo on page 1: Johannes Gutenberg checking pages
produced by the first printing press in Europe.

This book was produced for Crabtree Publishing Company
by Bender Richardson White.

Photographs and reproductions:
The Art Archive: Museo Civico San Gimignano/Alfredo
Dagli Orti: page 5; Santa Maria della Scala Hospital, Siena/
Alfredo Dagli Orti: page 7; Museo d'll Opera del Duomo
Orvieto/Gianni Dagli Orti: page 8; Bibliothèque des Arts
Décoratifs, Paris/Gianni Dagli Orti: page 12; Private
Collection/Eileen Tweedy: page 14; Private Collection/
Marc Charmet: pages 1, 22; Bodleian Library, Oxford/
Auct F 4 15 folio 27r: page 27; Palazzo Vecchio, Florence/
Alfredo Dagli Orti: page 28
The Bridgeman Art Library: Private Collection/Photo
© Rafael Valls Gallery, London, UK: page 7; Offentliche
Kunstsammlung, Basel, Switzerland/Giraudon:
page 9; Biblioteca Universitaria, Padua, Italy/
Giraudon: page 11; Private Collection/© Look and
Learn: page 16; Private Collection/The Stapleton
Collection: page 17; National Library, St Petersburg,
Russia: page 18; Palazzo Pitti, Italy: page 19; Musee
des Beaux-Arts, Marseille, France: page 20;
Bibliotheque Nationale, Paris, France: page 23
Corbis: Stapleton Collection: page 10 (bottom left)
The Granger Collection: cover, page 29
iStockphoto.com: pages 4, 10 (bottom right), 15, 31
Topfoto: pages 13, 21, 24, 30; The British Library/HIP:
page 25; © 2005 Charles Walker: page 26

Library and Archives Canada Cataloguing in Publication

Mullins, Lisa, 1981-
Science in the Renaissance / Lisa Mullins.

(Renaissance world)
Includes index.
ISBN 978-0-7787-4594-5 (bound).--ISBN 978-0-7787-4614-0 (pbk.)

1. Science, Renaissance--Juvenile literature. I. Title. II. Series:
Renaissance world (St. Catharines, Ont.)

Q125.2.M84 2009   j509.409'024   C2008-907899-3

Library of Congress Cataloging-in-Publication Data

Mullins, Lisa, 1981-
Science in the Renaissance / Lisa Mullins.
p. cm. -- (Renaissance world)
Includes index.
ISBN 978-0-7787-4614-0 (pbk. : alk. paper) -- ISBN 978-0-7787-4594-5
(reinforced lib. bdg. : alk. paper)
1. Science, Renaissance--Juvenile literature. I. Title. II. Series.

Q125.2.M85 2009
509.4'09024--dc22

2008052602

Crabtree Publishing Company

Printed in the U.S.A./112012/JA20121109

www.crabtreebooks.com   1-800-387-7650

Published in Canada
Crabtree Publishing
616 Welland Ave.
St. Catharines, Ontario
L2M 5V6

Published in the United States
Crabtree Publishing
PMB 59051
350 Fifth Avenue, 59th Floor
New York, New York 10118

Published in the United Kingdom
Crabtree Publishing
Maritime House
Basin Road North, Hove
BN41 1WR

Published in Australia
Crabtree Publishing
3 Charles Street
Coburg North
VIC, 3058

Contents

Rebirth and Discovery

The Renaissance is a name people use for a time period in history. It began in northern Italy in the early 1300s and lasted for about 300 years. The word "Renaissance" means "rebirth" in French, and refers to the revival, or rediscovery, of ancient Greek and Roman knowledge. The Renaissance was also a time of great change, especially in politics, art, philosophy, and the sciences.

Before the Renaissance

During the Middle Ages, the period of time that came before the Renaissance, studying science usually meant reading books by ancient Greek and Roman philosophers, especially Aristotle, and writing and arguing about what these books said rather than studying science itself.

Aristotle was an ancient Greek philosopher and scientist who lived in 300 B.C. Aristotle thought science should look for the causes of natural events and explain why things moved, worked, or looked the way they did. He also believed that all things in nature were made up of different combinations of four basic elements: air, water, fire, and earth. Each element had a place in the world where it belonged, and it always tried to go there. The element of earth was heavy, so it always moved downward.

To explain why an apple falls back to the ground when it is thrown up into the air, Aristotle argued that it is because the apple is mainly made up of earth, and earth's motion is downward. While Aristotle's explanation of nature does not make much sense to us today, it did to people living in the Middle Ages and to most people living in the Renaissance.

Aristotle believed observing nature was important, especially when studying animals and plants. One of his books, called Parts of Animals, *contains thousands of his own observations of fish and other sea creatures.*

*In the Renaissance, "science" included many more practices than it does today. Medicine, mathematics, botany, and astronomy were considered sciences, but so too were law, **theology**, magic, and philosophy.*

New Practices

In the Renaissance, scientists began to question Aristotle's explanations, including his ideas about the elements. Most scientists learned about Aristotle by reading books about him, not by reading his actual texts. During the Renaissance, Aristotle's works and other ancient texts were rediscovered and translated into Latin. As Renaissance thinkers read these texts, they began to dispute them.

During the Renaissance, most scientists believed they should study nature directly. Carefully observing, or looking at, the natural world became important for them.

Many Renaissance scientists believed that if their own observations were different from what ancient thinkers had believed, the ancients must be wrong. They trusted their own modern senses more than the opinions of other, earlier thinkers.

During the Renaissance, observation became the most important way to learn about nature. Scientists began to conduct experiments, allowing them to physically test their opinions and theories in a way that other scientists could copy, and see for themselves if a theory was true or not.

Science in Daily Life

In the Middle Ages, science was studied only in universities and in religious institutions, such as monasteries. Most scientists were either priests or wealthy nobles. In the Renaissance, more ordinary people became interested in science because there were more books available, and more people went to university. New observatories were built for astronomy, and large gardens planted for botany. Scientists also started giving public lectures on many different topics, for anyone to hear.

Life of a Scientist

During the Renaissance, it was mainly only men who could study science, and they had to be able to read and speak Latin because that was the language of schools and universities. There were not a lot of jobs for scientists, and most did not make a lot of money doing science.

Science at University

Most people who became scientists went to university. University was expensive, so most students were from wealthy families. University students were taught Aristotle's sciences, including physics and biology, as well as astronomy and mathematics. They were also taught how to write books and make arguments. The sciences were taught as part of courses in philosophy or theology.

Newer scientific ideas and discoveries were not taught in universities, sometimes because professors did not believe them and other times because these ideas were thought to be against religion. Students who wanted to learn these new scientific ideas had to hire teachers or practicing scientists outside the university. Some scientists were self-taught, meaning they were smart enough to understand the books they read without having someone explain them.

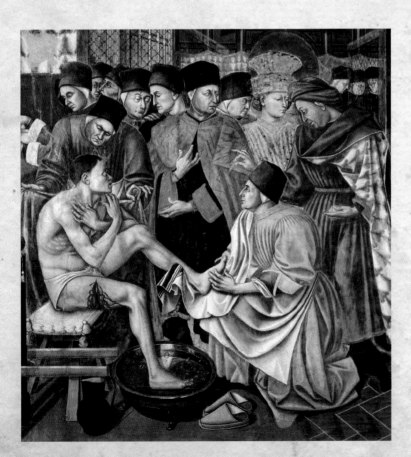

Medicine was the only science that made enough money to support a man and his family. Doctors could make a lot of money by treating the sick in a large city. Being a doctor paid so well that some doctors were able to take time off to study other sciences.

Apprenticeships

Not all types of science were taught at university. Some sciences, such as botany, engineering, and chemistry, were considered crafts, just like carpentry, shoemaking, and shipbuilding. These sciences were taught and controlled like any other craft, using the apprentice and guild system.

For example, the science of making medical drugs was a craft. Those who practiced it were called apothecaries. A boy hoping to become an apothecary entered an apothecary shop when he was a teenager. A boy's family would pay the apothecary to take their son as an apprentice and learn the craft. After about four years, an apprentice was qualified to join the guild of apothecaries. A guild was the group made up of all the people who practiced that specific craft in a specific city. Guilds made sure that all craftspeople had the same basic training and skills, and set standards for their work.

Earning a Living

Once a person had finished studying and training, it was hard to earn a living as a scientist. Aside from medicine, people in the Renaissance did not believe that the sciences were very useful. Most sciences were only starting to be studied and understood, and many people were not sure how their discoveries could ever be used in daily life. Scientists often had to have other jobs to make money, and did science as a hobby.

Many scientists were actually priests or church officials. These men did their regular jobs during the day, like leading church services or writing religious books, and studied the sciences at night. Some scientists were able to get jobs as professors at universities. They had to teach classes but still had time for their own scientific study. Other scientists got jobs with the army or the navy. Armies were always looking for new designs for weapons and armor, and began to realize that scientists could help. Large navies hired many scientists to teach their sailors how to use scientific instruments to **navigate** better.

Being an apprentice was not like going to school. Apprentices learned their craft very well, but they did not learn about any other science.

Patronage

The best possible job a scientist could hope for was at a royal court, under the system of patronage. Patronage was very common in the Renaissance. A wealthy, politically, and socially powerful person gave a scientist everything he needed to study and discover new things and to live comfortably.

In return, the scientist did certain jobs for his patron, such as giving advice to the military on new weapons. By having a famous scientist at his court, a patron showed others his wealth. The impressive work the scientist did helped the patron's reputation as a cultured and intelligent man. Kings and powerful princes would compete with each other to attract the most talented scientists, artists, writers, and philosophers to their courts.

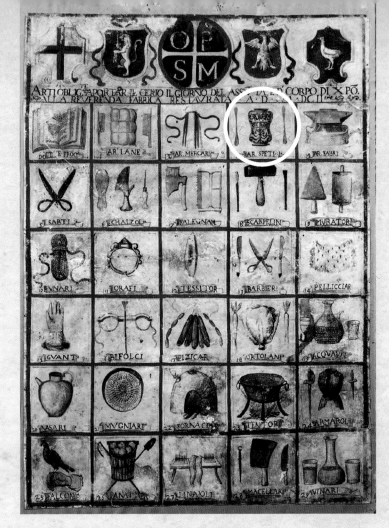

Each city guild had its own symbol. This chart of symbols comes from Orvieto in Italy. The apothecaries' symbol—a jar with two spatulas or blades—is circled above.

Women and Science

Some women did study and practice science, even though they were not allowed to go to university. A few noble women hired scientists to teach them about new discoveries. Some wealthy women had laboratories in their homes, where they did chemistry experiments and prepared and experimented with different medical drugs, most of them made from plants. At the end of the Renaissance, many wealthy women were interested in botany. They went out to the countryside and spent mornings collecting different types of plants. Women who were the daughters of craftspeople and merchants, and women who married them, also learned about certain types of science and technology while they helped in family businesses.

Gentlemanly Science

Some scientists were so rich they did not need to work at all. These men were nobles, who usually had the most books, the fanciest instruments, and the best places to work. Since they were rich, many other scientists wanted to be friends with them in the hopes of using their instruments and books. Noble scientists got to discuss the latest scientific work with all the most talented scientists of the time. Many were patrons to professional scientists. Most noble scientists considered their scientific work an entertaining hobby. Even though they were **amateur** scientists, they still made new discoveries in the different sciences.

Many teachers were also scientists. As the Renaissance progressed and science became more popular, some scientist-teachers were hired by noble families as science tutors. Tutors were given a place to live with the family and plenty of free time to do their own studying.

TIMELINE

1455: Johannes Gutenberg finishes printing the Bible, the first printed book in Europe

1492: The explorer Christopher Columbus lands in what is now the Bahamas, off the coast of Florida

1543: Mathematician and astronomer Nicolaus Copernicus argues that the Sun is at the center of the universe

1543: Andreas Vesalius publishes a new, illustrated guidebook to the human body

1545: First botanical gardens in Europe planted in Pisa and Padua, Italy

1572: Astronomer Tycho Brahe observes a supernova, or the explosion of a star

1590s: Spectacle-makers Hans Lippershey and Zacharias Jansen invent the microscope and telescope

1600: Medical doctor and philosopher William Gilbert publishes *On the Magnet*, in which he describes Earth as a giant magnet and names the North and South Poles for the first time

1605: Politician Francis Bacon publishes *The Advancement of Learning*, arguing that science must be done with a large group of people, each observing different parts of nature

1609: Astronomer Johannes Kepler publishes *A New Astronomy*, which describes the movements of the planets around the Sun

1610: Astronomer Galileo Galilei publishes a short book called *The Starry Messenger*. It includes drawings of the Moon as seen through a telescope for the first time

1628: Medical doctor William Harvey publishes his discovery of the function and movement of the heart, and the circulation of the blood around the human body

1637: Mathematician and philosopher René Descartes publishes his *Geometry*, introducing a new, simpler way of writing mathematical problems

Mathematics

During the Renaissance, mathematics was thought to be the most certain type of knowledge, because there was always a right and a wrong answer. More and more scientists started using math to prove their theories. Other people also became more interested in mathematics, as they realized it could make many tasks easier and the results more accurate.

Shapes to Numbers

During the Renaissance, people began to argue that everything in nature could be explained by math. The most important Renaissance mathematician, a Frenchman named René Descartes, believed that he could explain everything, from the movement of the planets to how flowers grow, using mathematics. He believed that our senses, like seeing and hearing, got confused, and gave us incorrect information. Descartes thought that mathematics was the only science people could trust.

In 1637, Descartes published an essay on geometry. The study of geometry answers questions of size, volume, and shape, for shapes such as cubes and triangles. To do geometry, mathematicians have to construct, or draw, shapes using instruments such as rules. In his essay, instead of drawing shapes and figures, Descartes showed how to do the same problems using equations. These equations took up less time and space and were easier to read. Mathematics still uses Descartes's way of writing equations.

Descartes's method of doing geometry was much faster. Most people found it easier to use, and his equations (below) were soon used everywhere.

$$3x^3 + 2x^2 - 6x + 2 =$$

$$x^3 + \frac{2}{3}x^2 - 2x + 1 = 0$$

Math for Everyone

Basic mathematics, like arithmetic and simple geometry, had always been taught in universities. During the Renaissance, mathematics was also taught in elementary schools and in different crafts. In cities, schools that taught just math were founded. One reason why more people learned math was because people believed it was necessary for many different jobs, such as navigation.

As businesses grew during the Renaissance, merchants needed better ways of keeping track of how much money they made and spent. Mathematicians invented tools to make their work easier and faster. One such device was Napier's Bones or Rods, designed by John Napier around 1600. Napier's Rods were a sets of rods with multiplication tables on each side. By arranging the rods in a wooden frame, multiplication was reduced to simple addition. All a person had to do was add up the columns instead of taking the time to multiply the numbers.

Art and Math

In the Renaissance, mathematics was useful in painting. In the Middle Ages, people in pictures looked flat, not three-dimensional, and their bodies were out of **proportion**. Renaissance painters used mathematics to make their paintings more realistic. They studied humans and animals, measuring the different parts of their bodies and writing down the **ratios** between them. They made sure they painted according to those ratios.

Perspective was invented in the 1400s in Florence, Italy, and is calculated using geometry. In a painting that uses perspective, the hills in the background are smaller than the people in the foreground, showing that the hills are far away. Perspective made paintings look more real, and people in them look more lifelike.

Many people at the beginning of the Renaissance could not do simple addition or subtraction. Some scientists did not learn the multiplication tables until they were at university.

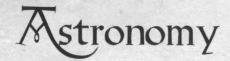

Astronomy

Astronomy is the study of stars, comets, planets, and of the universe in which we live. During the Renaissance, there were more important discoveries in astronomy than in any other science, notably about the movement of Earth and the other planets, and what the Moon looked like. Astronomical discoveries were used by people in different fields, such as by sailors to navigate.

Unmoving Earth

Until the 1600s, astronomy was based on the work of the ancient Egyptian astronomer Claudius Ptolemaeus, known as Ptolemy, who lived around the year 100 A.D. Ptolemy taught that Earth stood still in the center of the universe, and that the Moon, the planets, and the Sun moved around it. This system is known as the geocentric system, which means "earth-centered."

Ptolemy's explanation of the universe did not match astronomers' observations of the night sky. Some planets, like Mars, appeared to stop and start.

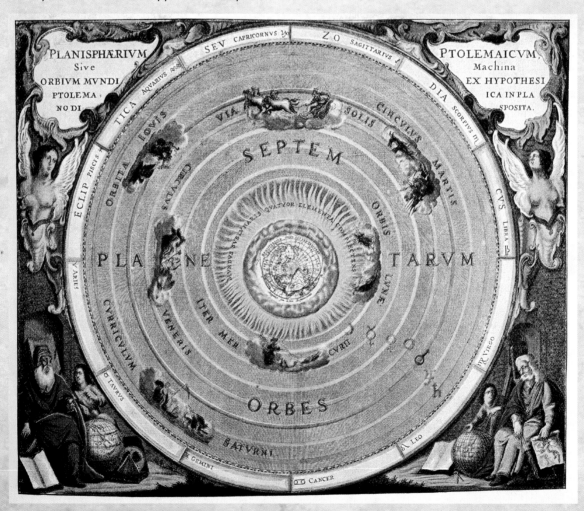

The Calendar

Since the early Middle Ages, the church had asked astronomers to come up with a good way to predict the date of Easter. Easter Sunday is the first Sunday after the first full moon after the first day of spring. Astronomers had to be able to tell the church when the first day of spring would be, and what phase the moon would be in years in advance, because the church planned the entire year based on Easter. In 1545, Pope Gregory XIII asked astronomers to fix the calendar. Christopher Clavius and Luigi Lilio wrote a plan, which the pope accepted in 1582. It became known as the Gregorian calendar and is still in use today. It is based on the movement of Earth around the Sun, and the movement of the Moon and the other planets.

A Spinning Earth

Ptolemy also thought that all the **celestial bodies** moved in exact and perfect circles. Ptolemy thought the universe worked this way because of Aristotle's science and also because of common sense. When he stood still, he could not feel himself moving, so he did not see any reason to suspect that Earth was moving through the universe.

Nicolaus Copernicus was a Polish priest and government official who was very interested in astronomy and mathematics. In 1543, Copernicus published a book called *On the Revolutions of the Celestial Spheres*. Using complicated mathematical calculations and some of his own observations, he argued in favor of a heliocentric, or "sun-centered," system of the universe. In his system, Earth

Until around 1700, Copernicus's view of the universe was not widely believed. Many clerics disagreed with him, since the Bible says that Earth stands still while the Sun moves.

and all the planets revolve, or circle, around the Sun, which is at the center of the universe. The Moon still circled around Earth. Copernicus believed his system was more correct than Ptolemy's because he could prove it with complicated mathematics. It also matched people's observations. Copernicus's system explained why Earth has different seasons, why days are sometimes longer than nights, and why the planets moved the way they did.

Tycho Brahe's Island

Tycho Brahe became interested in astronomy while he was studying law at university in Denmark. After he finished school, he built an observatory on an island off the Danish coast. Brahe made the most accurate astronomical observations at that time, using only his eyes, as telescopes had not yet been invented. He calculated the position of more than 800 different stars and made careful observations of the movement of Mars. On November 11, 1572, Brahe observed a supernova, or the explosion of a star. This convinced him that the heavens were not unchanging, as Aristotle taught, but Brahe still did not believe Copernicus's system.

Oval Movements

Astronomer Johannes Kepler worked for several different German and Austrian princes, mainly as an **astrologer**. He was one of Brahe's assistants, but believed in Copernicus's idea of a heliocentric universe. In 1609, after years of observations and calculations, Kepler published *A New Astronomy*. In this book, he wrote the first two parts of what are now known as the laws of planetary motion, or the rules of the speed and shape of planets' orbits. Kepler showed that planetary orbits were ovals, not circles. This movement around the Sun is called an elliptical orbit. Kepler showed that planets sped up and slowed down at different points in their orbits, depending on how close they were to the Sun.

Several years later, Kepler wrote a third planetary law, which used mathematics to compare a planet's distance from the Sun with how long it takes for that planet to complete one full orbit. Astronomers still use Kepler's laws of planetary motion today.

*Galileo's trial scared many scientists in Europe, especially in Catholic countries like France and Spain. They were afraid that the church would send them to the **Inquisition**, or that they would lose their jobs. For many years after the trial, scientists stopped writing that the Sun was at the center of the universe.*

During the Renaissance, astronomical instrument makers designed and made beautiful instruments, such as this astrolabe. One reason why astronomy became so popular during the Renaissance was because of the beauty of its instruments. Wealthy people wanted them in their homes because they were considered works of art, like paintings.

Galileo's Telescope

The Italian astronomer, mathematician, and physicist Galileo Galilei is one of the most famous people of the Renaissance. Galileo worked at the Medici court in Florence, Italy. He heard that spectacle-makers in Holland had invented a telescope and made one for himself. Using his telescope, Galileo saw many things no one had ever seen before.

In 1610, Galileo published *The Starry Messenger*, an illustrated book describing his discoveries. Galileo discovered that the Moon was not a smooth, perfect sphere but had an uneven surface, like Earth. He observed that the planet Jupiter had four moons orbiting around it. This was the first time anyone realized a planet other than Earth could have a moon. Galileo proved that the dark spots on the Sun were in fact on its surface and not clouds in front of it.

He also proved for the first time that the Milky Way is made up of billions of stars. His measurements showed that they were bigger and further away than people thought.

The Galileo Affair

In 1632, Galileo published *Dialogue Concerning the Two Chief World Systems*. In it, Galileo has three characters argue about the ancient Ptolemaic and Copernican systems of the universe. Galileo makes the character who believes in the Ptolemaic system sound like a fool. In 1633, Galileo was brought before the Inquisition and ordered to say that heliocentrism was not true. Galileo gave in and publicly denied Copernicanism. He was put under house arrest for the rest of his life, meaning he was not even allowed to leave his house.

Physics

Physics is the study of matter, energy, force, and motion, and the way they are connected to each other. It is an attempt to understand how and why things act and move the way they do.

Galileo's Falling Objects

In addition to astronomy and mathematics, Galileo also studied physics. One of the areas he was most interested in was the theory of motion. Galileo conducted experiments to disprove Aristotle's theories of motion. Aristotle believed most motion was caused by the four elements trying to return to their proper places. Motion happens at a speed that is determined by the elements, so objects containing a lot of earth will fall faster because earth is the heaviest element. For Aristotle, an apple, which has a lot of earth, falls to the ground faster than a feather, which has a lot of air but little earth.

Galileo realized, by watching ordinary objects roll down ramps and fall off tall buildings, that things move faster and faster the longer they roll or fall. Galileo believed it was the distance of the fall or roll that was important. He realized that all falling objects accelerated, or got faster, at the same rate as they fell toward the ground. It did not matter how heavy or light an object was, because every object picked up the same amount of speed. Galileo also discovered that a moving body will keep moving in the same direction unless something stops it. This is known as the law of inertia, and is still used today.

When Galileo wrote about his theory of falling bodies, he described the experiments he did to test and prove it. Historians have no records of Galileo actually doing these experiments, although he supported his theory with a lot of complicated mathematics.

Gilbert's book on magnetism was written in Latin. Many copies were printed and most scientists read it. Those who could not read Latin asked friends who could to explain it to them. The book included pictures of his experiments and of some of the very complicated instruments he designed.

Magnetism

William Gilbert was an English doctor who worked in London around 1600. In his spare time, he studied mathematics and physics and was interested in magnets. Gilbert was the first person to determine that Earth was a giant magnet, with a north and south pole. He called magnets "little earths" and believed that all the planets were magnets too. He said that Earth and the planets moved because of magnetism, an idea that no one had argued before. Gilbert's understanding of magnetism was very important for navigation and explorers because of the **compass**. Gilbert discovered that a compass needle did not point directly north. Instead, it pointed to magnetic north, a point on Earth that is not at the very top of Earth and does not stay in the same place. Gilbert devised an instrument to calculate the difference between magnetic north and true north. This enabled navigators to figure out their location at sea with much more accuracy and precision.

Shocks and Sparks

Ancient Greeks and Romans knew that rubbing a piece of amber with certain materials, such as wool, caused the amber to attract feathers and other lightweight objects. In 1600, William Gilbert, while working on magnetism, discovered that objects other than pieces of amber, such as diamonds, also attracted lightweight objects when rubbed with certain materials. He named this power "electric," after the Greek word for amber, which is "elektron." Other physicists began experimenting with "electrics" and discovered positive and negative charges. They learned that opposite charges attract each other, or stick together, while the same charges repel, or push away. Gilbert's discovery made electrical lights and batteries possible.

Medicine and Anatomy

When people in the Renaissance got sick, they went to the doctor to figure out what illness they had and how to get better. They suffered from ordinary medical problems, such as throat infections and broken bones, but also from epidemics, such as smallpox, which spread rapidly in crowded cities and killed many people.

Being Sick

Medicine in the Renaissance was based on the writings of Hippocrates and Galen, two ancient Greek doctors. They thought that the human body consisted of four different types of fluids called humors: blood, phlegm, yellow bile, and black bile. These four fluids made all the organs in the body. Renaissance doctors thought that illnesses and diseases were caused when the four humors were out of balance and there was too much of one and not enough of the others. People got fevers because they had too much hot blood, and stomach aches because something they ate made too much yellow bile. Doctors tried to restore a proper balance of the humors.

Medicine at Home

Most medical help was given at home, especially in the countryside. Every baby was born at home and delivered by female family members or by a midwife, a woman with some medical knowledge who delivered babies for a living. Many babies and their

Apothecaries prepared and sold medical drugs and remedies. Drugs were made out of plants, flowers, and chemicals, such as vinegar. They also sold ingredients for medicines so that people could make their own remedies at home.

mothers died shortly after birth because of infections from dirty water or clothes.

Every woman knew several simple medicines she could make from ingredients in her kitchen, garden, or farm. These medicines, like those that physicians prescribed, were made mainly from plants and animal parts. Mothers could cure their children of most illnesses, such as colds and sore throats. Most remedies were purges, made from herbs, which made a person throw up.

Treating the Sick

If a person got sick, they went to a variety of people for help, depending on how much money they had and what was wrong with them. A physician was a university-educated doctor, but he was expensive to visit. Physicians diagnosed illnesses by taking a patient's pulse and examining the color and clarity of their urine. They performed brief physicals and asked patients about their general health and diet. They prescribed changes in diet and more exercise, and sometimes recommended a drug.

A common treatment was bloodletting, which caused a person to bleed. Physicians either cut a person's arm to release blood or applied bloodsucking leeches, or bugs, to the skin. All treatments prescribed tried to restore the balance of humors in the body.

Barber-surgeons were members of a guild. They set broken bones, removed broken or infected teeth, and treated gunshot and other war wounds. They also performed surgery, cutting a patient open to try and fix internal injuries. Surgery was dangerous and few survived it. Surgeons did not have any drugs to put patients to sleep, so they were awake throughout the operation. People did not know germs existed, so surgical cuts got infected, or dirty, very easily.

The Plague

The scariest disease in the Renaissance was the plague. The plague was a very contagious and deadly disease that caused high fevers, bad coughs, and huge blister-like sores called buboes. Buboes burst open, bleeding and oozing puss. People in the Renaissance did not know how to cure the plague, and most people who caught it died. The only way to stop the plague from spreading over the entire city was to quarantine those who were sick or who had been in contact with sick people. Doctors were terrified of catching the plague, so when an outbreak occurred, they left the city.

During the Renaissance, hospitals became large institutions with beds for hundreds of patients, and many doctors, nurses, and surgeons. Many hospitals treated patients for free.

Anatomy

Anatomy is the study of the structure of any living body. The best way to learn about human anatomy is by performing dissections, that is cutting open dead bodies and studying their bones, muscles, and organs. Before the Renaissance, human dissections were not allowed because the church believed that dissection took away the dignity of the dead person. Galen never dissected a human, but he did dissect many animals. He based his human anatomy on the anatomy of dogs, cats, and farm animals. Since Renaissance scientists based their work on Galen, much of their understanding of the human body was incorrect.

In the later Renaissance, some cities had public dissections. These human dissections were very popular, with over a hundred people watching. They were educational, but also a form of entertainment.

More Bodies

Human dissections were introduced in universities in the 1300s, but only on executed criminals and only once or twice a year. Medical students were not allowed to dissect the corpse. They watched the barber-surgeon dissect, read their textbooks, and listened to their professor.

A big change in anatomy came in the 1530s when the Flemish doctor Andreas Vesalius started teaching at the University of Padua, in Italy. He argued that physicians and surgeons had to dissect human bodies to learn anatomy. Vesalius robbed cemeteries to get bodies to dissect for his students and himself. In 1543, Vesalius published *On the Fabric of the Human Body*. This illustrated book explained the real structure of the human body and how its organs, muscles, and bones worked.

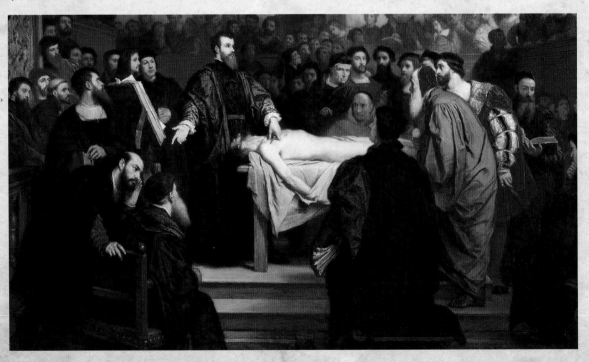

A Pumping Heart

The English physician William Harvey made one of the greatest discoveries of Renaissance anatomy in the early 1600s by discovering the circulation of the blood. By observing the hearts of dying dogs, he proved that blood moves around the whole body over and over again. He also discovered that the function of the heart is to pump the blood around the body, and that each side of the heart pumps, or beats.

Andreas Vesalius's seven-volume book, written in Latin and published in 1543, contained many detailed illustrations of human dissections and the different parts of the body.

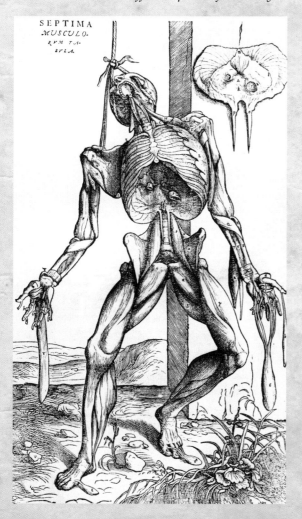

Art and Anatomy

Artists played a really important role in the work of anatomists. As anatomists dissected bodies, artists would draw very quickly the insides of bodies. Drawings were very important for learning anatomy, especially when students could not dissect many bodies themselves. Artists were happy to work with anatomists because it made their paintings more real. By studying the human body, artists learned how to paint humans better.

Changing Treatment

New discoveries in anatomy changed medical treatments. For example, the theory of the four humors and the treatment of diseases by bloodletting were disproved by Harvey's discovery of the circulation of the blood. Discoveries such as the structure of the human skull and how the intestines, liver, kidneys, and stomach were connected, led to improvements in surgery, because surgeons now had a better idea of where things were in the human body.

Surgery was still very painful, however, despite these advances in knowledge, and patients still died from infections. Eating spoiled food and drinking dirty water caused many of these infections, as did the lack of personal hygiene. Most people took baths only once a month, or as occasionally as once every three months.

Inventions and Technology

Many machines still used today were invented or improved during the Renaissance. Such inventions changed the way people did their jobs, making work easier and faster by taking away some of the sheer physical strength needed to get a job done. Most machines were not designed and made by scientists, but by merchants and craftspeople, such as carpenters and blacksmiths.

The Printing Press

The most famous invention from the Renaissance is the one people still use today. The printing press is a machine that speedily makes multiple copies of the same book, newspaper, or picture. Before the printing press, books had to be copied by hand, which took a lot of time and was very expensive. The printing press was invented in China between 500 A.D. and 700 A.D. In the 1440s, a German metalworker named

Johannes Gutenberg built the first printing press in Europe. He also invented a new way of printing using metal moveable type. Each letter and punctuation mark was made out of a tiny piece of metal. To print a page, Gutenberg arranged the individual pieces of type in the correct order. In 1455, 180 Bibles were printed. These were the first books to be printed in Europe and are now known as the Gutenberg Bibles.

The Arrival of Gunpowder

Gunpowder was invented in China in the 900s and arrived in Europe sometime around the 1200s. Before gunpowder, Europeans fought with bows and arrows, swords, spears, and catapult-like machines that threw heavy rocks against town and castle walls. With the arrival of gunpowder, Europeans could now develop new weapons, such as firearms and cannons, with a much greater destructive power.

By the 1600s, all the major European cities contained several large print shops. One printing press could produce more than 125 pages every hour.

New Weapons

Gunpowder was very unreliable, and not very many people understood how it worked. Sometimes a cannon would not fire after it had been lit, and other times it exploded unexpectedly. **Metallurgists** experimented with mixing different minerals and chemicals in with the powder to make it easier to light and safer to transport. Engineers also invented hand-held firearms, such as the musket, that one person could fire by themselves. They also developed guns for ships and created special carriages to drag larger cannons around a battlefield.

Renaissance engineers built gear and pulley systems for cranes that were used in the construction of large buildings.

DELL ARTIFICIOSE MACHINE.

FIGVRE CLXXVII.

Lenses

People had been wearing basic glasses since the late 1200s. In the Renaissance, spectacle-makers came up with new ways of shaping the hot glass and grinding it down. People got much better glasses because it became easier to make thinner spectacle lenses. In the 1590s, Dutch spectacle-makers Hans Lippershey and Zacharias Jansen realized that lenses of different thicknesses and which curved in opposite ways could be combined to make it possible to see objects far away. They created the first telescope, which allowed astronomers to see things they had never been seen before. They also invented the microscope, which enlarged small things like bugs and parts of plants.

Leonardo da Vinci

Leonardo da Vinci is famous as one of the greatest artists of the Renaissance, but he was also very interested in science and technology. From the 1480s onward, he invented many different machines. He designed several types of war machines, including a new type of cannon and cannonball. Leonardo was fascinated by the idea of humans flying, and so designed several flying machines that had giant wings that flapped like the wings of a bird. He also designed the first parachute, and a giant toy helicopter. Many of Leonardo's inventions were never built and existed only on paper.

Exploration

During the 1400s, Europeans explored the coasts of Africa and crossed the Indian Ocean to India. They also sailed across the Atlantic Ocean to North America and the Caribbean. During the early 1500s, they circumnavigated, or sailed around, the entire world. Scientific knowledge and instruments made these voyages possible.

Shipbuilding

The Portuguese were able to lead the rest of Europe in exploration because of their advances in ship design. In the 1200s, they developed the caravel, which was a light, fast, wooden, sailing ship. Caravels usually had a crew of 20 and contained a lot of cargo space for carrying goods back and forth to trade. Portuguese explorers realized that caravels were good ships to sail long distances in, as they were quick and could turn at speed. These were both important when exploring unknown lands, as sailors had no idea of what the coastline was like or where any underwater rocks might lie.

Larger vessels, called carracks, were also used because they were sturdy in the open seas and had room for crew and supplies.

Maps

Before the Renaissance, the size of Earth was unknown and no one knew how much of Earth was water or land. Maps in the Middle Ages were inaccurate, placing Jerusalem at the center of the world surrounded by only three continents. During the 1400s, mapmakers started to make maps, known as portolan charts, especially for sailors. These charts accurately showed the coastline, seaports, and harbors.

Renaissance explorers always traveled with more than one ship. Christopher Columbus's fleet of three ships included two caravels, the Nina *and* Pinta, *and one carrack, the* Santa Maria.

Latitude and Longitude

In the late 1400s, European mapmakers began to add horizontal lines on portolan charts, known as lines of latitude. These lines were numbered by degrees to indicate distance north and south from the **equator**. Mapmakers also added vertical lines to measure longitude, the distance east or west a ship had traveled. Soon, all maps showed lines of latitude and longitude.

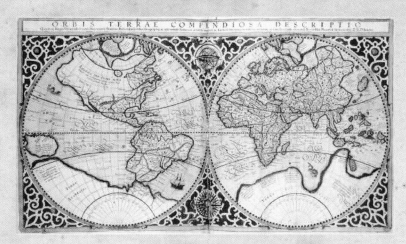

In 1569, Gerard Mercator, a Belgian instrument maker, made a new map of the world that was much easier for sailors to use than previous maps. He called it A New and Augmented Description of the Earth Corrected for the Use of Navigation. *Mercator's map became the model for all maps after it. Mercator's model is still used today.*

Instruments for Navigation

The most important instrument for Renaissance explorers was the compass, introduced to Europeans by the Arabs and later improved by William Gilbert. Its magnetic needle always pointed north, allowing a navigator to know which direction his ship was sailing. Astronomers helped navigators by teaching them how to use a quadrant. A quadrant measures the height of the Sun or a star from the **horizon**. From that, navigators could calculate their latitude. Astronomers also helped navigators to calculate longitude by making accurate maps of the stars. Navigators could look up at the night sky and work out roughly where they were at sea. Longitude could also be calculated by dead reckoning, that is estimating the distance a ship had traveled by calculating its speed over a period of time.

Columbian Exchange

The Columbian Exchange is the term used to describe the exchange of thousands of people, plants, animals, and diseases between Europe and the Americas that followed Columbus's voyages to the New World. For example, before the Columbian Exchange, there were no oranges in Florida, no cows or pigs in Texas, and no blueberries or strawberries in Europe. Serious contagious diseases, like smallpox, did not exist in the Americas before 1500. Smallpox killed thousands of native peoples in both North and South America. The Columbian exchange had long-lasting effects on both sides of the Atlantic that are still felt today.

Plants and Animals

Botany, the study of plants, and zoology, the study of animals, were both very popular during the Renaissance. European explorers in the Americas, Africa, India, and the Far East of Asia observed and brought back many new plants and animals that were previously unknown to Europeans. Botanists and zoologists tried to figure out how these new, strange living things could be related to European plants and animals.

Plants and Gardens

Botany grew in popularity during the Renaissance as many new species of plants were discovered and brought back by explorers. Botanists were curious about these new plants and examined them to see if they could be eaten or used to flavor food, or whether they had any medicinal use.

An interest in botany also inspired large gardens that were open to the public. The first botanical gardens were planted in Pisa and Padua, both in Italy, in 1545. These gardens were places both to study the plants and also to relax in the open air. The gardens were filled with ordinary European plants and flowers, as well as plants and flowers brought back from the Americas and India. Bringing in plants from all over the world allowed botanists to study them without having to travel abroad.

Animals

Scientists had always studied dead animals in order to understand their anatomy and compare it to human anatomy. In the Renaissance, scientists were very curious about the anatomies of new animals brought back to Europe. They were especially fascinated by the big lizards discovered in South America, because many types of lizards can regenerate, or grow new legs, arms, and tails if they get cut off.

In the mid-1500s, a group of German botanists published this herbal. A herbal is an instruction book, containing many detailed pictures, on how to grow plants, where to find them, and how to use them.

Bestiaries contained descriptions and illustrations of what animals looked like, where they lived, what their anatomy, diseases, habits, and diet were like, and any uses humans might have for them. Bestiaries also included information about imaginary animals, such as unicorns and dragons.

The Menagerie

Renaissance zoologists also observed living animals, which taught them much about how different types of animals lived, what they ate, and how they mated and gave birth. They were helped in their studies by the popularity of menageries, the Renaissance equivalent of a modern zoo.

A menagerie was a place where exotic animals were kept in captivity. Menageries were kept by royal or noble families in the gardens of their palaces or big country houses. These families wanted to show off their wealth and power. Menageries gave them the opportunity to do this, as exotic animals that were alive and active were very difficult to obtain and expensive to keep. The most famous menagerie during the Renaissance was kept in the Tower of London in England. The Tower Menagerie was open to the public and included lions, elephants, leopards, cougars, exotic birds, lizards, and many other animals.

Chocolate

One of the most popular plants discovered during the Renaissance was the cacao, or chocolate, tree. Chocolate comes from the seed of the cacao tree, which only grows in Mexico and South America. Native peoples drank chocolate as early as 1400 B.C., and cacao beans were often used as money in parts of South America. No one in Europe had ever tasted chocolate before Spanish explorers first brought it back across the Atlantic in the middle of the 1500s. It soon became a favorite drink at royal courts. At first, chocolate was extremely expensive in Europe and, until the 1700s, only rich people could afford it. Renaissance apothecaries, botanists, and doctors all believed that chocolate was very healthy, and used it as a type of medicine.

The Occult Sciences

In addition to mathematics, physics, and astronomy, science in the Renaissance also included magic, alchemy, and astrology. These sciences were known as the occult sciences, which means "hidden" or "secret" sciences. Magicians, alchemists, and astrologers thought they were studying the secrets that nature kept hidden, as opposed to the other sciences that study what can be seen.

Magic

Almost everyone in the Renaissance believed in magic and it was considered a type of science. Magic gave a person control over natural powers, such as the wind and rain. Using these powers, magicians believed they could make objects fly and cause other people to do things. Magicians controlled nature in different ways, mainly through chanted incantations or magic spells.

In the Renaissance, people believed that certain unpredictable events were caused by magicians. These events, like the appearance of comets in the sky or unseasonal falls of snow in the spring or summer, are of course caused by nature, but this fact was unknown to many people, who could not figure out what had caused them to occur.

Alchemy

Alchemy was an early form of chemistry. Like modern chemists, alchemists performed experiments by mixing and heating chemicals, such as mercury and sulfur, metals, and the leaves and stalks of plants. Alchemists were not trying to make medicines and new materials, as modern chemists do. Instead, they were trying to figure out how to turn poor-quality base metals, such as tin and copper, into gold, and make themselves rich.

An alchemist's laboratory was full of different equipment, including furnaces for heating mixtures, glass bottles for storing liquids, and big stone and metal bowls for mixing ingredients together.

People of all social classes believed in and used astrology. Royal courts employed astrologers to give advice about important government decisions and make predictions about members of the royal family.

The Philosopher's Stone

Alchemists were also trying to make the philosopher's stone, which was usually seen as a necessary ingredient either to turn metals into gold or else to make the elixir of life, a potion that could cure all diseases and make a person live forever. Many people distrusted alchemists, believing that they were greedy by trying to make gold for themselves. Most alchemists kept their experiments hidden from others, and wrote down their observations in secret languages and pictures so that no one else would be able to discover their secrets.

Astrology

Astrology is the study of how the positions of the Moon, the Sun, the planets, and the stars affect what happens on Earth and on how people behave. Astrology was extremely popular in the Renaissance. Many parents went to astrologers when their children were born to ask for a nativity or a geniture, a detailed chart showing the positions of the planets and the stars at the time of their child's birth. Astrologers read the charts and made predictions about what the child would be like and what would happen in its life. Some doctors also considered astrology to be very important for their work. These medical doctors were known as astrologer-physicians and were very popular in large cities, seeing thousands of patients a year. Astrologer-physicians and their patients believed that the stars and planets caused diseases, and that cures for these diseases were found by making astrological charts.

Religion and Magic

The church was not sure what to think about the occult sciences. Some practices, like astrology, were so widely used that even the church believed in them, although these sciences go against some parts of the Bible. Church officials thought most magic was bad and that magicians were somehow talking to evil spirits and demons. These magicians were arrested and many were killed. Other types of magic, like the healing magic that made sick people better, were good, and the church allowed these magicians to keep doing their magic.

Changing Lives

During the Renaissance, new scientific discoveries and inventions changed the way people thought about the world around them. New institutions were created in which the different branches of science were studied, leading to further discoveries. These discoveries, however, did not improve life immediately for most Europeans, although they did lead to many changes and improvements later.

New Stories

One reason why ordinary people were so interested in science during the Renaissance was because of the printing press. The printing press helped information and news to travel much faster than before. People in the Renaissance were very excited by new scientific discoveries. Authors wrote stories about traveling to the Moon and the planets and meeting extraordinary creatures.

Explorers returning from the Americas and elsewhere were treated like heroes. People could not wait to hear their exciting stories of how they had discovered new lands and what the peoples, plants, and animals of those lands were like. Exploration completely changed how people thought about the world. For thousands of years, Europeans believed that their continent was at the center of the world and was all the land that existed. They had no idea there were huge

Francis Bacon worked for King James I of England. He thought that universities should teach science differently. Instead of making students read books, Bacon thought university teachers should make their students do experiments and learn science that way.

continents across the oceans. As more and more explorers traveled from Europe to Asia, the Americas, and Africa, Renaissance Europeans realized there was a whole new world to discover, explore, and study.

Oxford and other old universities have collections of Renaissance science books and instruments. These items are valuable and often very fragile because of their age.

New Rules for Science

By the end of the Renaissance, new scientific discoveries were always in the news, and people wanted to learn more about science. One such person was the English lawyer and politician Francis Bacon. Bacon was not a scientist, but he was very interested in the sciences. He believed that observing and experimenting were the only methods to do science. He thought that nature could be understood only by working together with other people, and sharing what they learned.

Bacon wrote a book called *New Atlantis*, which was published after he died in 1626. *New Atlantis* is the story of an imaginary country, with a scientific institution called Salomon's House. Salomon's House is a huge organization, with teams of people carefully studying, experimenting, and observing every part of nature, such as the weather, astronomy, and different types of flowers, rocks, and minerals. It was a model of how Bacon thought science should be done. European scientists, especially in England, soon became fascinated by Bacon's method. Salomon's House became the model for the English Royal Society, the very first national institution devoted to science. Many scientific institutions today are still based on Bacon's methods.

Studying Old Science

Historians learn about science in the Renaissance from studying the different objects that have survived up to the present day. Thousands of old scientific instruments still exist, including medical instruments, telescopes, and microscopes. Many books about science written during the Renaissance also still exist. Renaissance science can also be studied by looking at manuscripts, or handwritten pages. Scientists kept notes of how they conducted experiments and what discoveries they made. Some of these notes have survived. Historians also study science in the Renaissance by looking at paintings done at the time, to see what clothes scientists wore and what their laboratories looked like.

Further Reading and Websites

Rees, Fran. *Johannes Gutenberg: Inventor of the Printing Press.* Mankato, MN: Compass Point Books, 2006

Steele, Philip. *Galileo: The Genius Who Faced the Inquisition.* National Geographic Children's Books, 2005

Koestler-Grack, Rachel A. *Leonardo da Vinci: Artist, Inventor, and Renaissance Man.* New York: Chelsea House Publications, 2005

Dawson, Ian. *Renaissance Medicine.* London, UK: Hodder Wayland, 2005

Elizabethan Science and Technology www.elizabethan-era.org.uk/elizabethan-science-technology.htm

Renaissance Connection www.renaissanceconnection.org

Teacher Oz's Kingdom of History—Renaissance www.teacheroz.com/renaissance.htm

Glossary

amateur Not professional; not experienced; unskilled

amber Hard fossilized tree sap often used in jewelry

astrologer Someone who studies the stars and planets and uses them to predict human behavior

celestial bodies The stars, planets and other objects seen in the night sky

compass An instrument that shows the direction north

Equator An imaginary line around the middle of the Earth, dividing it into northern and southern halves or hemispheres

horizon Where the land, or water, in the distance appears to meet the sky

Inquisition A church court that punished those whom it felt were doing things that were against the church's teachings

metallurgists People who worked with metals

monasteries Places where monks or nuns lived to follow religious rules or practices

navigate Finding a ship's course, position, distance traveled; finding the way to a place

observatory A building from which to watch something, usually the night sky

philosophy Study of the rules or truths to be found about life or the universe, studied by philosophers

proportion The measure of how two things relate in size

quarantine To separate or isolate someone or something from contact

ratios The measures of a proportional relationship between two things, written as two numbers separated by a colon

theology The study of religion

Index